JOURNEY INTO WISDOM EVERLASTING

Journey Into Wisdom Everlasting

from

THE EPIPHANIC ARCHIVES

KENN KNOPP

iUniverse, Inc.
Bloomington

JOURNEY INTO WISDOM EVERLASTING
...from THE EPIPHANIC ARCHIVES

iUniverse books may be ordered through booksellers or by contacting:

iUniverse
1663 Liberty Drive
Bloomington, IN 47403
www.iuniverse.com
1-800-Authors (1-800-288-4677)

ISBN: 978-1-4502-7211-7 (sc)
ISBN: 978-1-4502-7212-4 (ebk)

Printed in the United States of America
iUniverse rev. date: 11/11/2010

TABLE OF CONTENTS

FOREWORD

Proverbs 3:5-6... *Trust Yhwh with all your heart, and don't rely on your own understanding; acknowledge God in everything you do, <u>and God will direct your paths.</u>*

The scripture quotes herein have been taken from *The Inclusive Bible*, Rowman & Littlefield Publishers, 2007; 4501 Forbes Blvd., Ste.200, Lanham, Md 20706; http://www.rowmanlittlefield.com This bible, see above verse of Proverbs, uses the Jewish reference to God, Yhwh, not to be pronounced, but meaning Jahweh or Yahweh or "God the self existing." This gesture of Christian translators is most kind.

Our Theme comes from the Catholic Mass in which we are reminded, *"...count us among those You have chosen..."* Always be determined to stay in the State of Grace through the Sacraments (Communioning with Jesus, or the Doorways to Jesus) for it is Jesus Christ who knocks on the door of our hearts and minds in hopes we will open ourselves to Him and Divine Providence. Remember, there is no doorknob on His side. When you hear Him knocking it is your decision to open up the door to invite Him in. His purpose is to safely lead us to His Father in the peace and presence of the Holy Spirit and the great welcoming in heaven into the Church Triumphant. When Jesus calls (**Matthew 25: 3**) or comes again hopefully He will claim us as one of His own. *"...enter My Kingdom My good and faithful servant, enter into My joy!" (**Matthew 12: 21**)* Let us pray then that He finds us walking in Him and with Him and trusting in the Holy Spirit... which is Wisdom, the ultimate and never-ending gift of the Holy Trinity.

Here are some scriptural guideposts to help you "along the Way"...(suggested minimum daily requirement: 1 scripture search!): Genesis 6; 32; Numbers 21:5; 1 Kings 2; Isaiah 46:10; 64:7; 12: 29-30; Ecc.7:20; Proverbs 6; 12:27; 16:9; 14:29; 24:18; 29:8; 30:6; 30:33; Numbers 21:5; Psalm 111:10; Jeremiah 9:23; Matthew 12:28; 18:11; 26:39; Luke 7:21; 10: 21; 11:52; 14:27; John 1:12-13; 2:27; 3:1-3, 9; 3:16, 21; 5:21; 6: 20, 54; 63-68; 7:17; 9:31; 15:16; 44-47; Romans 1:15; 2:12-13; 7:15, 25; 8:28-30; Ephesians 1:4; 2: 10; Hebrews 9:15; 11:1; Phillipians 3:10; 1 Corinthians 10:16; 13:10; 15:29-30; 2 Corinthians 3:2-3; 1 Timothy 11:17-20; 5:13; 2 Timothy 3:16; 1 Peter 3:15; 4:2-3; 4:7; 2 Peter 2:12; 2 John 6; Galatians 4:19; 5:7; Titus 2:12; James 1:5, 26; Acts 3:15; Revelation 17:5; 18:1....

Please keep a *Daily Journal*. You will cherish for it years to come; and those who come after you will thank you. Make a special note of a scripture that especially intrigues you or may have caused you to pause. There is a cause to that pause!

INTRODUCTION

This compendium is offered by a Catholic deacon 35 years in the ministry but forced to retire because of health. We state this since the Wisdom word is often used by today's New Age and Gnostic adherents. We say that with respect, since, after all, God chose the Magi-Astrologists-Wise Men, outside of His Chosen Ones, the Jews, whose openness was such that they trusted the Star to lead them to a very special kind of new ruler: the infant Jesus, the Savior of the world. They acknowledged Jesus' specialness with precious gifts of their time.

In old-town Salzburg, Austria, across from the historic Stadtkrug Hotel is a pharmacy with a beautiful stained-glass inscription over its front door: *For Every Malady God Has Placed an Answer for It Nearby.* It is hardly believable that God would have created anything that does not have a purpose. How our selfishness has contaminated God's awesome creation that makes our hearts so hardened. God is determined to bust up our stony hearts and reconstruct us into the likeness of Jesus! The stories herein hope to give examples of how a caring God goes about this.

Our use of the word Epiphany comes from its meanings and uses in the Old and New Testaments of the Bible as proclaimed anew through Vatican II and subsequent encyclicals or special teachings. What we present, however, is not to be considered official or inerrant church teaching. These personal testimonies are called private revelations. To many they are quite hard to believe. To some they are quite inspiring. St.Thomas, whom Jesus chose to be one of his original twelve apostles, had a hard time believing anything he didn't actually experience or see for himself. The Magi or Astrologers from a far off country were moved, out of their belief, to follow the Star; which led them to the Savior they presented with gifts of honor. That was their Epiphany! They cooperated with God's Plan! Today's epiphanies also move along God's plans to ultimately fulfill His greater purposes. Even from evil God can make good things happen. It is a great theological statement that *evil should scare the hell out of us!* All creation has some sort of role to play in the Creator's Plan.

Our goal and hope is to provide insight, encouragement, and an opportunity to share examples of special experiences of unique grace, that is, favor from God. Such help or intervention of our heavenly Father can take place at any opportune moment, on God's part, in one's life's journey. Please don't think we are trying to make heroes of those whose stories are presented here. The real hero is our merciful God who tends to those in special need of guidance, reprimand, reformatting and encouragement. The church militant, the followers of Christ, silently and courageously receive sufficient strength to carry their daily crosses. Some grow in grace and truth without the need for an extraordinary epiphany or charism. Either way, God is gathering His church triumphant, the result of His handiwork.

We embrace fidelity to the Catholic Church and its bishops who have come to us through unbroken lineage since having been chosen by the Lord Jesus Christ and his apostles, the first bishops. This order or Magisterium, charged with safegarding doctrines and teachings through the centuries, helps to keep our journeys on the right road of the Savior whose purpose is to safely lead us to His Father and celestial life everlasting.

We love and respect our separated Christian brethren and pray that one day we will all come to realize that we have so much in common that we once again may be united as one. We're all claiming the right to sit at the foot of the Lord Jesus. We are grateful to Pope Benedict XVI for advising us to respect the traditions and particular practices of other Christians. We rejoice in the Personal Use Liturgies of some of our separated brethren that are now being accepted by the Catholic Church in full communion. Perhaps it will be these Epiphanies that will help somehow to bring about more unity in Christ Jesus and His Church.

God is always in charge, mercifully! The special event of an epiphany is often life changing, that is, causing one to change one's mind or to go in another direction. Though the event can sometimes seem brutal, ultimately it becomes a blessing and proof of God's love and mercy. Such epiphanies result in one's continuing the life journey with more humility and in a far more satisfying and fulfilling way. Like another chance! In short, Let GO! and Let God!

1 Peter 3:15... *Should anyone ask you the reason for this hope of yours, be ever ready to reply...*

Please share your moment of epiphany to help others also to be aware of God's ever-abiding Grace, or attention to a special need at a certain junction of Critical Mass of Life. The event is not always complicated; but can be... and sometimes even occurs to those whose rudders in the water of life are "steady as you go." (That is, not so splashy! Not all are given or need profound Charismata!--it is the Holy Spirit which knows the charism that is needed.) Please keep your report short.

We number the reports as we receive them and that will be your unique number. Our witness is about God's elect, that is, how He blesses them and keeps the blessings moving forward! We do reserve the write to edit your testimony to control the length, some grammar and some "big" or fancy theological words. Our goal is to edit in order to edify. Most of our readers don't have those special dictionaries handy. Let us know if you wish to remain anonymous. We need your written permission to use your name. Our policy is not to reveal names and actual locations. Once the story is placed on this website, we destroy the original email or letter, keeping actual details forever untraceable.

Email us putting in the Subject Line: **My Epiphany...**
alterstolz@gmail.com

-1-

the awesomeness of mercy...

I was in the service and was put in charge of a undercover assignment across enemy lines on a small ship during World War II in the Pacific. As the operation got under way I somehow did something wrong and caused the boat to be grounded. I was brought before the Navy court to be tried, the event was considered to be anathema. However, after the judge looked over my training and schooling, which was a spotless record, and no previous violations, after a long and silent while, he suddenly dismissed my case with a warning that he hoped he would never see me in the courtroom again. Everyone was stunned because he had the reputation of being the most stern of all the Navy judges. I was more than stunned... and left the court just amazed, and most grateful. I had just been to Mass that morning and had prayed that I might receive some sort of mercy. But I had not expected that much mercy. I had several promotions and one day I found myself in the position to also be a sort of judge. I got the reputation of being very fair and "merciful".

I now know my God is one of Mercy. My daily prayer to Jesus is: *"Lord be merciful to me, a sinner."* **(Luke 18:13)** My Christian walk as a follower of the Catholic Way is to try to stay on the Path of Mercy... as my journey continues.

-2-

...an angel leads me to the Way & the Truth...

Thanks for letting me share. I had been living in the French Quarter in New Orleans as an artist for a number of years; and am not Catholic. Although I was baptized in a Protestant Church I was never confirmed or attended church. Coming to New Orleans was fascinating, including becoming involved in Voodoo activities, the drug scene, etc. I found it exciting and mysterious as well as some of the persons I met at the black magic shops. One such lady convinced me that I should present myself for what she called "cleansing aroma therapy." It was some kind of ritual she performed while I relaxed, and even sometimes dozed off. For days after, I dabbed at bathing for fear the interesting aroma might leave. I never had so many girlfriends. But one particular lady friend insisted I change my "after shave lotion." She was revulsed about the Voodoo cult in the French Quarter; and changed the subject whenever I brought up black magic. She was a Protestant and said she would pray "for my deliverance." So I began splitting up my time, sometimes with her, other times with "the other." Months went by, and I became quite torn apart. Finally she told me to decide: her and going to church with her, or stop seeing each other. I was so repulsed by her closed mind, but I called her bluff and broke things off. She never called me, despite me being so irresistible. The next few days one bad thing happened to me after another. I began to get a bit morose and bad tempered. Even my paintings were being rejected. And I could see why. I passed by a chapel and stopped for a moment. All I noticed was a red lighted candle holder. I never took my eye off the flickering candle. The pure air and stillness baffled me. But was soothing. I don't think I even knew how to pray. But, my Protestant girl friend's image came to my mind; real strong. That night I called her up and apoligized and she agreed to meet me for Cajun coffee at the 'du Mond. I was amazed how we got along.

We decided to stick together and we moved to San Antonio her hometown. She is my guiding light; well, my angel. The Voodoo stuff seems to have been snuffed out. If she invites me to go to church with her I will. I am sure that I had some sort of Epiphany thing. By the way, my painting sales are increasing at the quaint shops along the River Walk and La Villita. Things are looking up; and I thank God for sending me my 'lil angel!

-3-

... Proverbs 15:16, pray for God to lead you and He will!

Christopher, this space will remain dedicated to your walk! As a young college student interested in the Great Books and the Fathers of the Early Church; and about to go sojourning to Europe and Rome this summer, our prayer is that you will have Encounters that will prove to be very meaningful to you in your spiritual growth and your coming career (we call your Calling.) Don't worry about your report to us. Your response to God is what counts! Hint: He wants you to be reformatted, that is Christ-centered. If God so chooses it may be some years before we hear from you for maturing spiritually sometimes takes time; or, if God chooses, shortly. Remember God does not want you to be ignorant, or, stupid. He has His own a way of letting you know the Right Way... and which is always hand in hand with Christ Jesus. Blessings to you as you go on your own very unique Way! No one else was created like you and your purpose to perform. All the best in Christ!

-4-

Our road of life was planned by God ages and ages ago....

Thanks to Ilse for emailing us with this testimony of God's Grand Design she found in *The Curate's Diary* by Fr. T. Doyle*:*

In 1920 a 43 year old German policeman was getting concerned that he had not met the right woman to marry. In desperation he placed this ad in area newspapers:

Middle ranking civil servant, single, Catholic, 43, immaculate past, from the country, looking for a good Catholic, pure girl who can cook well, tackle all household chores, with a talent for sewing and homemaking, and a view to marriage as soon as possible. Fortune desirable but not a precondition.

A lady named Maria Peintner answered the ad. She was 36 years old, a trained cook, born out of wedlock. While carrying her, her mother, whom it is suggested was also born out of wedlock, spent some time in a home for pregnant girls. The mother later married a baker with whom she had five daughters, including Maria. Maria did not have a fortune but she herself was a treasure. She married the policeman four months later. In spite of their somewhat advanced years they had two boys and a girl.

The youngest child received the same name as his father: Joseph Ratzinger, better known today as Pope Benedict XVI. After his election to the Holy Office someone dug up the "wife wanted" advertisement and showed it to the Pope. He smiled and added that they were the best of parents to their children. He knew his parents really loved each other and the children very much. In fact, his first encyclical was entitled *God is Love* describing marriage as the preeminent example of God's love for humankind. Even being illegitimate every child is a gift....and a possibility of being chosen to carry on The Epiphany of God's love!

-5-

a white dove, a sign sent from above...

It was late in the day as I was driving back to Dallas to get some rest after another day as a traveling salesman. I spotted a large bird ahead of me right in the middle of my lane of the highway. Surely it would fly off as I got closer. But it didn't. I drove right over it, to my great distress. I looked back and it was still sitting there. So I backed up to it, a white dove, to see if it was dead, or if not to get it to fly away from the road. Just as I stopped to get out of the car, it suddenly flew away. "What a silly exercise in futility!" I scoffed at myself as a waste of time. I went on my way and reached the Dallas motel where I would be staying for two nights.

Early the next morning I heard scratching at my door. Puzzled, I opened the door and sure enough it was a white dove with a lame leg. I asked at the front desk if there was a veterinarian nearby and there was. The vet agreed to keep the dove to try to fix it. I told him I couldn't keep the bird and gave him 10 bucks for his trouble, to which he agreed.

The next morning was a Sunday. As I was reaching for a newspaper a lady also approached the newsstand. Her nose was horribly disfigured. I greeted her and she greeted me. She began to speak saying she was from Phoenix and had an appointment the next day with a cancer doctor. I told her I would pray for her. Then she asked me if I believed in miracles. "They do happen." I told her. She asked me if I knew where she could go to pray for such a miracle. I had heard that the Dominicans had a parish that was charismatic and they had a prayer group with the laying of hands and healing services. But I had never been to one of those. Then she asked me if I could take her there. A bit stunned, I agreed. Looking up the address it was in the Dominican high school gym near the Dallas suburb of Mesquite.

So I took her there. Have never experienced anything like it. A small orchestra, lots of singing, spontaneous praying, scripture reading, a priest preaching, and then testimonies followed by break-out rooms: newcomer questions, scripture study, baby care room, special prayer room for healing, and a coffee-donut room for fellowship and chit-chatting, etc.

We went into the special room for praying for her healing. Five or so persons were ahead of my lady friend. When it was her turn the core group gathered around her and began praying in tongues and what not. Then all of a sudden one of them asked the group to stop praying: she had a revelation or Word of Knowledge that the lady had a deep hatred of someone in her family and more prayer would not be called for. I was flabbergasted and wanted to get up and leave. Suddenly my lady friend turned red with embarrassment and said that yes she hated her new son in law; and that he would not obey her wishes. The more he rejected her demands the more she turned on him. It was all a mean mess. The core group lady then asked her if she would forgive her son in law and try not to boss him around anymore. She responded that she would and would do her best to cut the meanness out, and that she didn't realize how things had gotten so out of hand. The core group lady hugged her and asked the group to then continue to pray for the healing of her cancer-eaten nose. The prayers were intense; and my lady friend went out of there beaming with joy. It all scared me nearly to death. I was glad to get out of there. The impertinence upset me.

But, about a month later I got a telephone call from that lady from Phoenix. The cancer had gone and the nose had built itself back up. She claimed she was healed. She and her family were Methodist but they started going to Bishop Brophy Prep Prayer Group in Phoenix. Her son in law also started going to the prayer group and was asked to play his guitar in its music ministry. They were getting along great. All in praise of their God Who Heals!

Here is an example of two epiphanies at one time: for I got the point, too, when I found out that the White Dove represents the Holy Spirit. The dove on the highway was probably the good Lord testing my sensitivity to ministry. I then started going to a nearby Prayer Group too. And lo and behold I received the gift of Praying in Tongues, just the thing I so disliked at the Dominican Prayer Group!

Editor's Note: *After doing some googling, come to find out that the prayer meeting was held in the gym of Bishop Lynch Prep in East Dallas. The preacher was the noted Dominican theologian and writer, Father Paul Hinnebusch, O. P. He died in 2002 which indicates the lady with the cancer and friend had gone there some years before Father Hinnebusch's death. The prayer group still exists, has its own building, and is called The Christian Community of God's Delight, 4500 W. Davis St., Dallas TX 75211. Tel: 214-333-2337, and meets on Sundays at 4 p.m. Bobie Cavnar was the founder of the group and is a nationally recognized Catholic evangelist. The "coincidents" of this story are quite amazing!*

-6-

Angels Unawares...

For several years I had been getting more and more depressed, that is, distressed over my grown up daughter and a son. Their situations keep on getting worse and I feared I would crash before they would. I just can't get them to go to Mass or to make a visit before the Blessed Sacrament. We live out in the country about 75 miles from the city with shopping centers. One day I made the trip into the city to shop at the Payless Store. I went over to a clerk who seemed to be an interesting person and asked her where a certain item might be.

The clerk was most pleasant and we talked for a bit. Then she added that she noticed when I came into the store that I might be carrying quite a big burden. I acknowledged that this was true. Then she surprised me by suddenly assuring me that God was already taking care of things and heard my prayers; and that I would soon have reason to praise Him. "I hope so" I replied and thanked her for the encouragement as I went on my way.

A few weeks later I received a call from my daughter to find out that her problem involving a large amount of money had been resolved. Then a few days later the son called letting me know that he had been promoted and that things were looking up. Both of them even thanked me, knowing that I had been praying for them night and day and fretting twixt and between. I said a rosary in thanksgiving. Then it came upon me that I should go to the city and tell that nice clerk my good news. I arrived at the store and went to the checkout stand where she had been. But she was nowhere to be found. I asked the manager what had happened to the lady...and described her as well as I could remember, telling him I don't think we ever exchanged names. He answered that no such woman had ever worked there and that he hadn't had to hire clerks recently, and his clerks had been working for him for years and years. He insisted I was at the wrong store. No, I knew this was the right store. I also once had heard about "angels unawares" and concluded that the store clerk had to be a messenger from God to keep me from falling into deep depression and to build up and strengthen my faith. I pray now with much more confidence..and thanksgiving!

Angels Unawares? See **Hebrews 13:2**, *Don't neglect to show hospitality to strangers, for in doing so some people have entertained angels without knowing it.* (it seems God sends angels as messengers to certain people when a person in the vicinity does not have the gift to do what the angel would then do.)

-7-

entities fill places where God is not welcome ...

My husband and I were very happy when we learned that his grandfather had willed him the family house out in the country. We had two children in their twenties who had already left home. We had tried and tried but have not been able to have any more children even though we wanted at least one more child very much. We enjoyed moving in to the country house. But things got to be a bit odd right from the start. In the bedroom one picture of the grandparents we liked very much and wanted to leave it there. But it kept falling down to the side no matter how often we set it straight. I would straighten it out one day, and next day find it hanging sideways again. Also, our family cat would come into the room and then suddenly start screeching and run right out of it. We both also began feeling very uncomfortable in the room, but couldn't figure out why. We finally thought we were just too wound up from the surprise of getting the house and being able to live in the country.

We would talk about how uncomfortable we were in the house; which came as quite a surpise to us. We had visited Oma and Opa often years before and never once got the idea that something might not be right with the place. Then it came to me and I asked my husband, "Have you ever known why Oma & Opa never went to church or never prayed at mealtime? They never questioned why we went to church and raised our children in the Sacraments. Could the house be haunted by something or another?" "Maybe, I don't know. But something is going on. I will make some inquiries..."

They contacted friends who were active in a prayer group. In a few days members of that group came to their house. After awhile the leader suggested they pray in each room and sprinkle each room with blessed Holy Water from church to claim each room for Jesus Christ. They said the Lord's Prayer, the Hail Mary, and the Glory Be, and in stern terms... *"that those presently living in the house were now believers in Christ and intended to always serve the Lord Jesus. If you are a Fallen Spirit or of the Evil One you should leave this place as you would be not be comfortable here anyway. We ask you to leave this place at once in the name of the Father, the Son Jesus, and the Holy Spirit!"*

We thanked the group for their prayers and hoped for the best. The next morning we were awakened very early by our cat. That was shocking because the cat never came in our room and to our bed before. We were stunned. Also, the picture was in its place and was hanging correctly. And, we felt different. We noticed more fresh air. I got on the phone and called my prayer group friend immediately. Could the prayers have been answered? Weeks went by and everything was completely normal. Not only that, I found out that I was pregnant. That did it, me and my husband now really do believe the scripture and say it often: ...."*as for me and my house we shall serve the Lord!*" (**Joshua 24:15**) We do not want to have a spiritual vacuum in our home as happened to our grandparents who stopped going to church for so many years. Jesus is the center of our family!

James 4:7-8 ... *Submit yourselves, then, to God. Resist the Devil, and it will flee from you. Draw near to God , and God will draw near to you.*

the healing of a memory

Gina and I, Anna, decided that we would make the 300 mile trip to Glorietta Encampment in New Mexico for a weekend retreat to be given by an order of nuns, the Disciples of the Lord Jesus Christ, whose motherhouse was at Prayer Town near Amarillo, Texas. Gina wanted to deepen her relationship with Christ. I needed that too; but I thought it would be a very fun trip no matter what. What a beautiful area for a retreat. At the camp there were several hundred participants and everyone was very friendly. Greeting us was Mother John Marie whom we found out was even the founder of this group of sisters. We each received a schedule which included daily Mass followed by breakfast, a general welcome, and then a chance to pick from number of topics and presentations. I told Gina I was attracted to one of them, *The Healing of Memories.* She said she seemed to like that one also, so we found the building and took our seats.

The lecturer was a professional in either social work or psychology and a practicing Christian. She described how someone might experience a mighty jolt, usually negative, by someone or something, in their life. It could happen any time in someone's life line, young or old. Sometimes the event would be so jarring or shocking that the person could not assimilate it properly; or, refuse to accept or process it, allowing it to sink deeply into one's subconscious as a form of repression.

Then she began a very peaceful and deeply thoughtful prayer asking the Holy Spirit guide her through an imaginary person's birth beginning with the Eye of God and forming the baby in the womb of the mother. She prayed about the love the couple had for each other which had created the setting for the child that would soon be born. She went into details of the parent's personalities, even their differences. Even in the case the family having little funds to support the new child that their love, sacrifices and dedication would get them by. Then the presenter went through details of childhood and relationships with siblings as well as good times and bad times in the family. Did anyone remember their first day going to school? What about teachers as well as the fellow students? Did anyone remember anything in the classroom, or at recess, or on the way home after school?

The presenter then gradually made her way into the teenage years and graduation and the college years; time to look for a job, and very importantly, their relationship with parents and others doing those years. How did they do in their relationship with God and their church from First Communion until the Sacrament of Confirmation, and as young adults, and into their twenties.

Perhaps she then assessed the ages in the room and brought the review of possible memories to a conclusion. She then thanked the Lord for the gift of memory and any recollection that might be stirred up. Sometimes the memory was not at all pleasant and might call for forgiving or apologizing to someone. Or, perhaps a most pleasant memory popped up calling for more expressions of appreciation and thankfulness toward someone special, or particularly God. In conclusion, she asked us to share any specific memories with her privately in an adjacent room. She then dismissed the group after a prayer of thanksgiving.

Gina felt very good about the session but said she did not recall a memory that might be out of the ordinary. To my great surprise, I was different. I remembered vividly when I was in the 5th or 6th grade in school when my teacher announced that we would all write a nice poem to our parents and bring it to them; perhaps thanking them for something they had done, or how good it was to have them as parents. My father was no longer living; but my mother just happened to have her birthday that same day. I wrote a poem for her. It actually rhymed. The teacher liked it and encouraged me to give it to my mother.

After school when I got home I was all smiles and gave the poem to my mother and wished her a happy birthday.

She read it; and read it again. But then she put the paper down and started scolding me: *You did NOT write that! You should not lie to me. Don't you ever do that again!* I tried to convince her that I did write it; she could even ask the teacher. But she just shrugged and went to do other things. Sometimes she would get that way, so it was not that great a surprise to me. I went next door to play with a neighbor friend.

Only when the event popped up in my memory at the retreat did I realize that perhaps it did have an effect on me, maybe trying to prove I could do something or another well; and in the process perhaps I had become an over-achiever. Now I felt sorry for my mother, rather than bitter, and was determined that from here on out I would try not to let her upset me. I lifted her up in prayer asking God to please bless her and give her peace. Through the years I have also thanked God for the sisters at Prayer Town, Texas, and the good work they do giving retreats and helping individuals, such as myself, in having a better relationship with parents, friends, and with God.

-9-

receiving our celestial bodies...

I would like to tell you about a dream I had. In the dream I was walking down a country road when I saw a person way down the road walking in my direction. We got within a distance that I thought I recognized him, a friend of mine named Frank who had died from cancer about five years back. Now within hearing distance I said, *Frank, is it you?* To which he answered, *Yes, it is...and how are you doing?* I replied: *I am fine;* but, I could not figure out if I was seeing things, I blurted out: *and how is it that you are able to be here?* With that he smiled... and I suddenly woke up. I could still see Frank as clearly as I did in the dream.

Sitting on the edge of my bed I was amazed that Frank looked so vibrant and much younger than the 60 year old when he died. I knew him as having very little hair; yet now he had a full head of hair. He had uneven teeth and was missing some when I knew him; yet in the dream he seemed to have all his teeth. In addition, I noted that I knew him to be gaunt or thin, but in the dream he was quite filled out. He was quite a talker; and I was convinced that he pestered God into letting him see for himself that I was okay. I got to see that he was fine! And, my faith in something I had been taught some years ago was also affirmed in that dream: that when we die to this earth we then receive new celestial bodies for the heavenly realm.

-10-

my guardian angel dear!....

My name is Mariechen. This happened about fifteen years ago when I was driving with my two daughters, ages 12 and 15 then. We were heading home just after dark following grocery shopping. The quickest way home was to use the Interstate Highway for about ten miles. Suddenly the car started making a spewing sound, began slowing down, and I was able to steer the car to the shoulder of the highway. I prayed, *Lord please send your angels to keep us safe out here.* Then there weren't any cell phones and I always feared car trouble on the highway especially at night time. I realized I needed to take my children by the hand and walk to the closest house with lights on. Certainly I should not let them stay in the car by themselves as I went for help. So I prepared them to come with me and told them to always hold on to me tightly and not let go.

Just as I locked the car and we were about to walk off, a large white van with two large men in it drove up. I began to get the shivers. But as they got out of their vehicle I couldn't help notice how very handsome and reassuring they were. They were dressed in all white uniforms. One of them greeted us and said, *We would like to help. Please release the hood latch and we'll take a look and try to see what's wrong.* I flipped the latch and immediately got the feeling that God had sent them. They worked for a bit under the hood and then closed it. *Nothing serious, just a loose connection. You can be on your way.* I asked them: *Are you angels?* They smiled, got in their vehicle, waved goodbye and drove away.

Still to this day I am convinced they were angels. God had answered my prayer and wanted to protect us. What else would God have created angels for if not also that! How that strengthened my faith. I thanked God over and over again. Now I am a grandmother and am still giving thanks. Sharing this story is also a way of continuing to thank my heavenly Father.

-11-

so filled up with self, no room for blessings...

Even though this story is fiction it it was sent by email and relates an important lesson that God is concerned about each and everyone of us.

Ol' Jacque lived along a Louisiana bayou and lived on fishing, crabbing and what not. He had an AM-FM radio that was on most all the time. One day came an urgent weather alert telling listeners a violent storm was coming and all should seek higher ground immediately. Jacque was busy with processing a large alligator he had caught and just ignored the alert. The rain started coming down in bucketfulls. A neighbor drove up to his house and called out for him to grab a few necessities and to come with him to a country school house that was on higher ground. "Naw, I'll be OK. Merci anyway!" (Merci = thanks)

The river was rising fast and had come halfway up to Jacque's house. Then a motorboat almost came up to his front

steps, *"Get in, we need to get out of here!" "Naw, I be fine." So
the man in the motorboat sped away.*

*Ol' Jacque started carrying things up to his attic. The rain
kept coming down in sheets. He opened the attic window and
crawled out on the roof. He heard the loud noise of a helicopter
and a voice over a loudspeaker telling him to grab the rope
connected to the bucket seat and get in the seat and hold on
tight. But, Jacque just waved the helicopter off.*

*Next thing he knew Ol'Jacque found himself standing
in the Foyer of Heaven. There before him was God Himself
standing, Jesus sitting to the Father's right in the Judgment
Seat, and a beautiful White Dove-- the Holy Spirit, perched on
the top of the Judgment Seat. Jesus spoke, "Welcome to heaven,
Jacque. That's the Good News. But the bad news is that since
you did not use the Grace, Truth and Knowledge we sent you
but instead turned down the people we sent to help, you are
going to have to spend some time in Purgatory to get you ready
for the wonderfulness of heaven. You were most always a good
neighbor and did what you could to help others. But we didn't
want you to obey only the Ten Commandments; we wanted
you to mature in your faith and commitment by putting into
action or becoming the Beatitudes. (see Matthew 5:3-11;
Luke 6:20-22).*

*Accepting the help or generosity of others is a beatitude. We
sent you the weather report first; then a neighbor to give you a
ride to higher ground. And, years before our Associate here, the
Holy Spirit, put it into the mind of the building committee of*

the school to be sure to build it on higher ground in case of a bad flood. Thankfully, they listened to the Spirit!

Then finally we sent a helicopter to rescue you. To be ignorant is excusable. But to be stupid, with your good common sense, may not be a mortal sin but certainly is a sort of venial sin, especially after all those people went through to help you. So, we have a special place for people like you in Purgatory. You will have a chance to apologize to every one in your life whose help you turned down for this and that part of your ego, pride. Then, finally realizing how stupid you were, then you will be prepared for the wonderful joys of heaven."

Lesson: Don't be so filled up with your own "stuff"---that you have no room for blessings!

-12. A-

God hears the cries of His people.....

My name is Julie Arizola of Fredericksburg, Texas, and am pleased to praise God by sharing these experiences. One dark winter night I was returning home to Fredericksburg after visiting family in San Antonio. Suddenly a great dense fog set in and I could hardly see ahead of me. I began to be afraid and it seemed like I was the only one on the road. I prayed, "Lord, help me. I'm scared and need your protection." As I was going up a hill and then going down into a valley ever so slowly, I saw the bumper or back lights of a car in front of me. I was able to follow the car. But we were about to come to the Fredericksburg turn off from the Interstate Highway, I feared the car in front of me would be going straight and was not going to take the turn off. But then the car turned its blinkers which signaled that it was indeed going my way. "Thank you, Lord" I exclaimed. I continued to follow the car when all of a sudden the fog lifted. The car in front of me turned onto the right shoulder; I passed it making a thank-you wave. Then I noticed the car made a u-turn and went back the way we came. *Was that car being driven by an angel? Truly God is always with us, listening to our thoughts and prayers, even in our darkest moments!*

-12. B-
the beautiful lady was an angel!

My late husband, Robert, and I used to operate a restaurant. One day, about to close, I could not find my glasses. I could hardly do anything without those prescription glasses, which were quite expensive. I especially needed the glasses to drive. What am I going to do? We didn't have the money at that time for new ones. Various things were happening in our family and our costs and expenses had skyrocketed.

We were about to leave the restaurant for the day when a beautiful lady came in. She was in a hurry and needed to continue on her way but she was very hungry. We talked a bit, she ate, and left. A little later I went over to the table where she had been and discovered that she had forgotten her glasses. She had paid in cash, with no way to make contact with her; and was long gone. Maybe she would come back. I tried on the glasses only to find they were exactly my prescription. I expected to get a call from that lady or that she would return for the glasses. But nothing ever happened. *I believe that lady was an angel sent down by the good Lord to help me. Praise God!*

-12. C-

God lets angels drive trucks!

From the Piney Woods of East Texas... My five year old niece and I were spending the weekend with relatives, enjoying their home cooking, chatter about this and that... when all of a sudden a weather alert was sounded about a weather storm that was brewing in the area. Since we had already delayed our departure once already I decided we should pack our things in a hurry and go. We would be heading in an entirely different direction than the storm. Rushing we hugged and kissed and jumped in our van and headed out. The storm area included about fifty miles and with a little bit of luck we would be able to evade it, or so I thought.

It wasn't but about ten miles out that we ran right into the storm. I ordered my niece to jump in the back seat and cover herself up entirely with a blanket and not say a word. I told her I needed to pay total attention and not to talk. Then the heavy rain started coming down, howling winds causing many pine cones to come crashing down on the car window. This was followed with hail. Fearing the worst I prayed and then prayed again.

In front of us appeared a large truck going very slowly. "If he can make it, so will I, if I stay close behind him." I told myself. "And if he pulls off to park on the side of the road so will I." Luckily after awhile we came out of the storm which was heading in another direction. I flashed a 'thank-you' blinker to the truck driver when we were able to pass him up and continue on our way. But I stopped when I came to a filling station and coffee shop. The clerk told us that from where we came out of us a huge tornado had hit; we were lucky to make it to his station.

When my niece was 30 years old I asked her if she could remember the Piney Woods storm so many years back. She answered, "Auntie, you didn't know it but under that blanket I was very scared." I replied, "Me, too! I feel that God had a hand in keeping us safe. It must have been a truck driving angel who we followed into safety!"

-13-

with God everything is possible. (Matthew 19:26)

George retired in the Texas Hill Country and chose the location because of its great golf courses, landscapes and weather. He likes to poke fun and make light of "things religious" and insists that he is not a "church goer." Another person in his coffee group who has the gift of Word-of-Knowledge asked George this question one morning, "George, has anything mysterious happened to you involving spiritual things which you just dismissed as "coincidental"? He grinned and then answered:

"Well, when I lived in Houston one of my coffee buddies there was a preacher. He had invited me, more than once, to come to his church on Sunday. I thanked him but told him that it would have to be one hell of a rain storm to keep me away from the golf course on a Sunday.

One morning the minister asked me what he should preach about for his next Sunday's sermon. Just joking and wanting to be cute I quickly said: "Leviticus Chapter (?) and Verse (?)." I don't remember the actual chapter and verse I told him. I just made them up on the spot. The minister jotted down the scripture and then excused himself to go to work on his sermon. That weekend it got cloudy and the rain began and wouldn't end. Still raining on Saturday night, I told my wife that since it was too wet to play golf, why not go visit the minister friend's church Sunday morning.

The minister welcomed us with open arms and was pleasantly surprised. But no one was more surprised than I was when the preacher announced that he had a special topic that was taken from Leviticus Chapter-- and Verse--. After the service the preacher said that the good Lord must really be after my soul, since He had performed two miracles: the scripture from Leviticus, and the downpour of rain to keep me off the golf course. Then I added another miracle: getting me to go to church!

-14-

what you do for the least of these you do for Me (Matthew 25:40)

Thanks for the Healing of Memories testimony (#8). Maybe mine is one, also. I recall in 1952 when I graduated from Catholic high school and later that summer enrolled in the University of Texas at Austin. Completing registration I was eagerly awaiting the first day of classes. Near my boarding house was the Night Hawk Restaurant, very popular with students for its bargain-priced generously sized chopped steak and fabulous strawberry cream pie. I had placed my order. Then coming in and sitting next to me at the counter came an Afro-American. I was proud to see him as it brought to mind the nuns teaching us Catholic social justice principles and our obligation to fight segregation every way we could and at all cost.

Just as my food was set before me the manager came up to the African American and told him gruffly that he must leave the restaurant. The manager didn't even offer him a seat in the kitchen or the storeroom. The black man silently got up and went out the door. I was mortified and left completely speechless. I was so ashamed of myself for not objecting or at least walking out with him. I invented all kinds of excuses. Would I have been kicked out of college on my first day of school? I thought about how much my parents had to borrow to send me to school. That event has never left my memory. Across the street from the restaurant was St. Austin's Church run by Paulist priests who also were in charge of the University of Texas at Austin Catholic Student Center nearby. I went inside the church, wrangling with my moral weakness and asked the Lord to help me do better.

It did not take long for more testing. I felt I had to leave the Republican Party because the Democrats seemed to be more sensitive to human rights and ending apartheid in the U.S. Then when Lyndon B. Johnson led the crusade to pass the Civil Rights Act my conversion to the Democratic Party was final. After college came the Medicare bill. The place where I was working was against it; so I flat upped and quit and found work elsewhere! I went by St. Austin's Church and facing the crucifix I asked Jesus if I was making up for my inaction years earlier at the restaurant across the street. Years later, national health insurance caused even more concern and will hopefully be more equitable to one and all. Then there's the need for immigration reform and a better Guest Worker Program. There seems to be no end to social injustice. I am convinced that Conscience, correctly formed (or re-formed in Christ) is also an Epiphany, like the Star of Bethlehem, or God's angels! I pray to be on the right road on my life journey.

the Mary and Martha Syndrome; *choose the best part, put yourself into the hands of the Lord!* (Luke 10: 38)

Two significant events in my life had the effect of reinforcing my beliefs and humbling me at the same time. They reminded me that God's plan for me are His to choose; and that I will always do better to be still and listen. It took many years, and crosses to bear, for that to finally sink into me!

A. The first event happened to me as an airplane pilot while flying an antique plane over the mountains of Nevada. The overcast layer of clouds and the desolate landscape rendered the world in absolute darkness. I knew there were mountains under and in front of me but I could not see them.

Suddenly the engine on the plane failed and without power the plane was going down. The runway lay beyond the mountains. My training spoke to me: if an engine quits I should glide down to the best landing area to be found.

But it was too dark to see anything. If I were higher than the mountains I would have seen the runway lights. There was only darkness which made me feel I would not clear the mountains or reach the runway.

Sensing imminent death I experienced a few seconds of sheer fright. Thoughts began to race through me such as who would care for my young children. But there also came an answer: I was safe and in God's hands whether I lived or not. But from within me I began to say the 23rd Psalm out loud. I got only as far as "The Lord is my Shepherd" when a sudden rush or sense of peace settled in and around me. I felt as if I was able to curl up in God's hands and be safe. This feeling has never left me and has brought me peace and joy at any number of crucial times in what I consider to be an extraordinary life. Amazingly the runway did come within sight and I was able to land safely. For me it was life-changing to feel God's physical presence which continues to sustain me, as well as being able to share this confidence with my family and others. Sometimes they look at me rather strangely for that.

B. In October of 2001 my 3 year-old grand-daughter Emma was dying of cancer. I tried to pray "God's will be done" but I don't think I really meant it. I hoped by saying the right words I could have my will be done and keep that beautiful child in this world. When she passed on into heaven I could scarcely breathe. For me the world had stopped. Her parents, too, just could not accept it. But, we believed in the resurrection and we felt we should all be together on that wonderful "rising up" day. We decided to find a special burial place on our beautiful Hill Country ranch near Doss, Texas, and to also build a small chapel at the site. As we were looking for the right location we noticed a swarm of bright yellow butterflies at a serene tree-filled knoll. Never in over ten years had I seen such butterflies. I had seen black butterflies and Monarchs but never pure bright yellow butterflies that were encircling a fifty foot circle on the little hill. God had chosen the place! Three days later we returned to the hillside where we placed her body that had held her soul and spirit. Friends and family sent beautiful flowers. And to our amazement God sent more yellow butterflies to the area. We gave thanks to God even though it was still very difficult to find peace in our hearts.

Deeply within me is quite a bit of stubbornness, my old nemesis. On Christmas Day that same year, despite a temperature of 25 degrees Fahrenheit and high winds, there came a surprising swarm of the bright yellow butterflies. We just sat there and cried. I took that as a sign of comfort and encouragement. Yet, I was still harboring resentment over Emma being taken away from us. The butterflies returned but in fewer and fewer numbers. I sensed that God was helping me in spite of my resentments. Continual problems followed me in my family and my career. I felt that God might be dealing with me and my traits of stubbornness. I was able to find solace there at the ranch knowing that God was attending to me. Now there came new butterflies advising and encouraging me, special friends and associates that I know God had sent to me. Year by year my stubborness seems to be abating. I am getting better at letting God in and "being still and listening" which is hopefully changing my heart in a way that pleases God.

(This beautiful testimony was sent to us by Linda Finch whose amazing life story can be found on the internet search by entering her name. She resides at her ranch outside Fredericksburg, Texas, and operates a personal health system specializing in weight control headquartered in Fredericksburg, a part of the SpaCityTexas Program. See http://www.SpaCityTexas.vpweb.com)

-16-

You will protect me from trouble and surround me with songs of freedom! ... **Psalm 32:7**

Julie Arizola's report (#12.A) helped me to recall a somewhat similar incident I had as a book salesman in the Panhandle of Oklahoma a number of years back. I had finished a call at Southwestern State University in Weatherford and was then heading out to 270 West for lunch in Woodward before pushing onward and calling it a day in Guymon. My next school was Panhandle State University in Goodwell the next morning about 15 miles south from Guymon. In Guymon there was a comfortable motel with a great steakhouse restaurant, making the lengthy drive a worthy goal to achieve that evening.

Winter had been turning into Spring and there were evidences of still unmelted patches of snow here and there along the highway. About twenty miles away from Guymon I came upon the top of a ridge. From the top of it in the far distance I could see the town of Guymon. Probably not knowing it I might have stepped on the gas pedal in anticipation of nearing my destination. As I was entering the very long and gradual descent down into the valley just past Optima Lake there was suddenly before me a large snow slick on my side of the highway. I suddenly lost all knowledge of what happened next. It was if I was in a complete suspension, totally blank, as my car started t o spin and spin around at least three complete times.

As I was sitting there in the car dazed, it quit spinning and stopped on the correct side of the highway. I knew instantly I should take the steering wheel, keep it straight and step on the gas to go forward; which I did. A car then passed me; and a car was coming toward me. I slowly increased speed not wanting to hold up any traffic. But I was still in shock, feeling faint, and totally amazed that the car had stopped spinning in the right lane and was still heading in the right direction... and without involving other travelers! To me that in itself seemed to be a miracle.

I looked up to the rosary hanging from the rearview mirror and Christ on the crucifix. I thanked the Lord over and over again as I entered Guymon's city limits. Approaching Main Street I noticed a church steeple and continued in the church's direction. It was St. Peter the Apostle Catholic Church. With weak knees I entered the church and plopped down on the first pew I came to. Again I expressed gratitude to the Lord and if there were any of his mighty angels also assisting in the incident He should please give them my thanks. After a bit I was breathing regularly and left the church making use of the Holy Water at the front door with the sign of the cross and proceeded to drive across town to the motel. After a good rest, I enjoyed the steak and again thanked the Lord for seeing me through that time of trouble. I think I now understand St. Peter's fear in that boat and his fear or the approaching storm a little better now. The only difference is that I didn't have the chance to call out for the Lord's help, it all took place in a split second. But, then again, maybe the good Lord was with me in the car as He was with Peter in the boat. I also realized because of these types of things, my faith had grown little by little as had my confidence and trust in the Lord.

-17-

from the Holy Spirit came the precious gift of Hope!

My wife and I decided to go to the Colorado Rockies to get out the Southern heat and the dog days of the summer. What a beautiful drive through the Big Bend, varying landscapes, deep gorges and over rivers, deserts and the majestic Rocky Mountains. Coming to a nice little city we stopped at a western style hotel that struck our fancy. We checked in and went to our room hoping to relax for awhile after the long drive. As I entered the room I immediately smelled a strange odor. We agreed to turn on the air conditioner and leave to let the room freshen itself up. We would not mind having our evening meal a little early; perhaps first driving around town a bit.

The hotel clerk told us about a popular cafe that was famous for its freshly caught river trout. It was great. After the nice meal we went for a little walk along the river's edge. We agreed we had given the air conditioner in our hotel room enough time to get refreshed. Returning the air in the room had sufficiently cleared, we relaxed, watched the news on TV and then went to bed. The long rest would help us have a vigorous day the next day.

Next morning the wife shook me urging me to get dressed to go the gathering room where the hotel was serving a Continental breakfast. I could barely respond. She could see I was in trouble and could hardly breathe. She went to the front desk and asked the clerk for the closest ER or a doctor. He said such services were lacking in the little town and that we should quickly go seventy-five miles to Denver. Or, if it appeared very serious he could call 911 and the EMT would come right away. He went on to tell her about the National Jewish Hospital in Denver and its world class pulmonary clinic and fine reputation. She paid the bill, thanked the clerk, and within a few minutes we were on the way to Denver. The clerk had also given us a Denver map and marked the quickest way to the Cherry Creek area not too far from the hospital. It turned out to be a straight shot.

An attendant rolled me into ER faster than I've ever experienced before. I was getting weaker and weaker but could still express myself adequately. Before the doctor came to look me over two nurses hooked me up to the drip thing, gave me a shot of something, and a breathing treatment. I shouldn't leave out the taking of some my blood. The ER doctor examined me and asked me to try to nap because they needed to wait for the results of the tests. Meantime, ex-ray came in and took pictures.

My wife seemed assured; and that helped me, too, as I tried to snooze. After awhile the doctor returned to let me know that it was thought I had caught a vicious dose of Legionaires Disease, something like "cytomegliavirus", or the summer flu. He added that things would not be getting better for me because whatever I had was still in the initial attack stage. He recommended that after stabilizing me as they could, we should immediately start our way back home. Halfway they would recommend a physician if I took a turn for the worse. But, if possible just go on to our city in Texas because it had one of the best doctors there for this type of thing. They would fax my medical data to him. But I should go straight to the emergency room there. He ended by saying that what I had caught was very serious. If his guess was correct it would be the same thing the members of the American Legion had caught at a hotel in Philadelphia. Some had died because of contaminated air conditioning. We stayed the night in the ER room. Feeling a bit better but extremely weak the next morning, we ate what we could for breakfast and then left that great hospital and headed for our home down in Texas.

It wasn't an easy trip stretched out in the back seat of the car; and going to the restroom at a number of truck stops. But we pulled into the ER of our hometown hospital where they had already been alerted by the Denver doctor. I was rolled past the ER onto an elevator to a room in the regular treatment wing of the hospital. We had heard much about our famous doctor in our hometown but it was our first time to actually meet him. Just one glance at him and we knew he was filled with great knowledge and insight. He told us he would do his best; but that it would not be an easy thing to treat. I promised him I would do my best, too. My wife added that her best would be to pray, pray, and pray some more! She got out her rosary. We smiled. The doctor just before departing told us, *You've heard where there's a will there's a way; but it would be better to say, never give up hope! Again, let's all do our best!"*

It would be several years of treatment in the hospital, home health attention, pulmotherapy, and then repeat all over again. The priest made regular visits at the hospital and in our home. He, too, agreed that we should not cease to pray to God for more Faith, HOPE, and Love. There's was that word again! Hope. Never before had I given much attention to "hope." Now, though, it had become a curious mystery of a word for me. Eventually the priest told me I had the "gift" of hope because he noticed I had never shown any sign of fear or despair though the doctors implied that I very well might not be able to pull through. Serious pneumonia would always be stalking; such are the mysteries of the virulent superbugs of today.

I have never really completely got over what the doctor always calls "exacerbations." But, I have some great moments and a few days from time to time of feeling good enough. One of the deacons in our parish brought me this prayer after I told him about the fixation I was having with the word "hope." That prayer has sustained me; hopefully even to the inevitable day it would be my turn to enter eternal life:

In the name of the Father, the Son Jesus, and the Holy Spirit: My God, I hope in You for grace and salvation, because of Your promises, Your goodness, Your mercy and Your power. Amen

-18-

a good deed, is good indeed!

Let me bear witness to something that happened to me when I first got out of college and found my first job in Houston. I called up a good friend, Gene, a most dynamic person who had graduated a year or so ahead me. He had landed a fine executive position in one of those tall skyscrapers in downtown Houston. We met for lunch and enjoyed reminiscing. He then asked me about the work I had been hired for. I told him that it was a great opportunity as a representive for a sportswear company throughout the state. Another friend had had the job and was doing well in it. But his wife couldn't stand him being away from home sometimes a week or so at a time. He then had to find something else. His company asked him if he could recommend someone he knew. He recommended me for the job; and after the interviews they offered me the position.

But then I went on to explain, I was still driving that little second hand Simca car I had the last two years of college. I was afraid it would not be able to stand being on the road so much. *"That's no problem"* my friend Gene responded. *"I'll just give you the keys to this car. Our car pool is bigger than a football field. One of my duties is being in charge of the fleets. When you start making enough commissions that you can buy or lease one of your own, just let me know and we'll pick this car up." "Really?"* I responded completely overwhelmed. I dropped him off that his office building.... and drove off with his car. Unbelievable. A cousin was living in Houston. I called him to ask if he was interested in my old Simca... for free. He jumped at the offer. (After all, one good deed deserves another!)

It was a good and different feeling not to be the "taker" and to be the "giver" for once in my life. A few months later in Austin I found a good looking second hand Oldsmobile I could lease for $125 per month. I telephoned my friend Gene in Houston and told him I was ready to give his car back. Delighted, he said that he and a friend would be in Austin by noon the next day. I treated them for lunch and tried to give Gene some thank-you-cash; but he flatly refused as they left to go back to Houston.

Sadly, Gene died of cancer about a year later. I guess he was just too good to have to wait any longer for heaven. I have always thought that if he didn't make it to heaven I probably wouldn't stand a chance! But, being still here on earth, I was being given more time to build up my good deeds account.

...it is said of St. Francis of Assissi that when sending his pairs of friars out to do good deeds among the people he blessed them and then added this admonition: *Always remember, the best sermon you can give is often one that is without words!*

-19-

who gives orders to the wind and the waves and they obey Him ... St. Luke 8: 25

Many years ago, during my work in Central America I fell in love and took for my wife a beautiful young lady from Coban, Alta Verapaz, Guatemala, very near the border of Mexico. Coban is a fascinating place for me being a German American. For over a century Germans (from Germany) set up coffee plantations in the area. The Dusseldorf family still operates a large coffee plantation there as well as many other endeavors that bring much needed work to the people there.

We enjoy visiting my wife's people there and relaxing in the beautiful little city and the wonders of nature in the area such as the Semujc Champay park. But, there is a place of special miracles we try to make a pilgrimage to in Esquipulas, the Basilica of Our Lord, which was recently voted as the most important edifice of all Central America. My wife had many a prayer answered through the years in that awesome huge white cathedral. She says the Lord answers her prayers more speedily there! We are so grateful for answered prayer. For that we give the Lord all the honor and glory. But, what we also would like to share and give God even more glory for, is how He has protected that venerable 400 year-old church despite tornados, hurricanes, floods, and what not.

Awhile back we all became quite frightened because a fierce hurricane warning was announced in all the media and from home to home. It was called "Mitch" and was scheduled to hit the Basilica of Esquipulas and the town directly. We prayed that we and the church might be spared. As the storm approached everyone was amazed it stopped before reaching the church, went straight up and then completely passed over the church and the town. But it did much damage as it continued inward into Guatemala. Certainly God Himself had again spared that holy church where we have been blessed as well as thousands of others. God tends to us. We appreciate the opportunity to share this testimony.

... whom even the wind and the sea obey... **St. Mark 4:41**

-20-

Phillipians 1:1, 2:2... *If our life in Christ means anything to you... be united in your love with a common purpose and a common mind...*

As a Lutheran pastor, a student of Christology and church history I have always been appreciative of Martin Luther's desire to bring reform to the Church in the 1500's. How sad that the reformation caused splits in Europe and then in England. We have all come a long way in working for the day of reunification of the Christian Church. Vatican II brought us all a great sense of hope and joy especially in the employment of the language of the people rather than clinging to Latin. St. Francis of Assisi likewise caused great waves when he confronted the Catholic Church in pleading for reform and calling attention to the urgent needs of the less fortunate. His confrontation before the pope in pleading for reforms and understandable liturgy did not cause him to be excommunicated as happened to Luther; or such a bitter reaction from those in power. Nevertheless, one must always take a stand for what is deemed right under the light of Christ. Both Luther and Francis, from their varying perspectives with the grace of God paved the way for us today to enjoy much agreement, respect and brotherhood with one another.

If each of us would do what we can unity might proceed. One thing I have often thought about is that we Lutherans, on our part, might give Mary the mother of our Lord more attention, perhaps with a hymn in her honor. That's it! I would introduce such a hymn during our Sunday worship service. I was sure it would be well received, well, by most of the congregation. I gave the Catholic deacon in our town a call and asked him to pick me out such a hymn or two to chose from. He was glad to do so. But, after looking them over I had to call him back and explain that I felt compelled to skip the idea. The hymns both included asking Mary "to pray for us." ..."no other mediator than Jesus" I explained to the deacon. He replied that often someone in his parish or someone sick or needing prayer had asked him to pray for him or her. "Certainly I didn't tell the person to go straight to God...and leave me out of it." the deacon said.

In the end I decided it was still too risky to do a hymn about Mary or "to" Mary. Instead, I chose to begin the worship service by telling the congregation that I had never liked the idea that the Catholic Church had the dubs on making the Sign of the Cross; which belonged to all Christians from the earliest times to the present. Why not show that we loved Christ and the Cross as much as they do. At the service I asked those in attendance to join with me in honoring Christ and demonstrating our Christian unity by making the sign of the cross with me: "In the name of the Father, the Son, and the Holy Spirit. Amen." There were no complaints. Except one lady after the service told me she thought I might have done it backwards! I was lefthanded!

Perhaps that moment did not qualify as an Epiphany event or a manifestation of Christian unity. But I have an inkling that real unity will come about as a great Epiphany or manifestation of the triumph of the Holy Trinity; in juxtaposition of the Tower of Babel. We've all done our babeling long enough! The wonderful history in the Bible revealing the unity of the Holy Trinity, Three in One, should inspire all the divisions of Christianity to pray fervently for real reunion, communion and reunification. Perhaps the good faith I might be looking for is the day when the Catholic Church might give the honor due to its Augustinian monk, Martin Luther... if not sainthood! What an Epiphany that would be! (All this said in faith, hope, charity and peace!)

(Editor's note: What a joyful manifestation of Epiphany it would be if more unity would come about amongst the Christian denominations. We appreciate this Lutheran pastor's yearning; and we pray for unity along with him. We have mentioned in our introduction of this compendium about Personal Use liturgies sanctioned by the Catholic Church when a Protestant pastor and some of his congregation wish to be received together into the Catholic Church. In some cases, the pastor becomes a priest and is even married. You can read about this by internet searching "Our Lady of the Atonement Church, San Antonio, Texas" received into the Catholic Church in the San Antonio Archdiocese without having to lose its Anglican tradition.)

-21-

a prediction & prophecy... the writing on the wall...

The date of my email to you is 8-9-2010. It concerns a dream I had in vivid technicolor. If the dream becomes a reality this email would be proof I did give a friend of mine in the car business a warning or help the dream compelled of me at a time of great stress for my friend.

There was a large sign (*the writing on the wall!*) in front of his car dealership: **Hybrid Fill Up Station**. *Park & Ride Our Loaner Car As You Do Your Business!* Several car dealers in our city had lost their dealerships because of the 2010 recession and the down sizing of their number of dealerships. My friend was the first car dealer in the area to erect electric and gas fill up connection ports. In the front of his dealership he no longer only had his dealer brand but now there were all kinds of makes: new models and used cars. His service and car repair area was now doubled in size.

In his large back lot were rows of ports or stations for filling gas, electric connections, battery charge ups and other ways to "fill up" the many makes of hybrid cars and trucks. It reminded me of the rows and rows of connection ports in our RV parks. As I pulled my hybrid/gas car up to his Service Kiosk I was given a card that was punched with the Time-In and Date. To charge up my car fully would take two hours.

After being given the key to my Loaner Car the attendant drove my car to the port-station where my car was plugged into the electric hookup. He then let me off where my Loaner Car was waiting. I drove off happy as a lark to go to the bank and pick up things at the local Farmer's Market and the pharmacy. About three hours later I returned to the car dealership, turned in the ticket and paid the bill. My car was waiting in the front row... all recharged up and ready to roll! A week or so later after the dream I felt I had to share it with my car dealer friend. I felt it my duty to do so. I told him that if he put the dream into reality and the venture was a flop, the dream was of the devil and he would have the right to put me to death by stoning! But, if it was a success, we would both praise the Lord with a great big hoot and holler! Will this come to pass?

-22-

whom the Lord loves He chastens.... **Hebrews 12:6**

A friend gave me your internet address and recommended that I read the experiences of persons about special moments in their lives. I had told her about the special event that had just happened to me. But, not belonging to any Christian denomination, I did not give the happening any more significance than being a wake-up call or a grounding process. In my way of thinking it was a mercury retrograde occurrence. So here goes:

I prefer not to give my name since I am at a rather mature age. If my grown "kids" read this they would probably insist that I no longer drive a car. That would just devastate me! But, let me go on with the story. I drove myself the 400 mile trip to be with my grand-children for a week since their parents are not able to get much time off to come visit me. It was a most wonderful time; though quite exhausting. Each day was a different experience. It filled me up with lots of love and sharing; and I feel the feeling was mutual. One of my daughters had recently died and I felt I needed the closeness of the family to help me continue the process of getting through her sudden and tragic loss.

Driving back to my home along the busy and boring interstate highway and reaching about the halfway point to my home, I began feeling hunger pangs and sensed that my blood-sugar was inching too low. I took the next exit seeing strip-stores and a restaurant over the way a bit. After driving down the side road and coming to an intersection I thought I needed to turn left to reach the restaurant.

I made the left turn and lo-and-behold I found myself going the wrong way on a one-way street and about to crash into the front of an oncoming police car! Fortunately I was not going too fast and was able to step on the brakes. I'm sure the policeman was as stunned as I was about the near head-to-head collision. He pointed me to park on the shoulder. He asked me for my driver's license. I told him I had no idea I had entered a one way street. He told me that it was a miracle no one was injured. He was patrolling the road because it was a road noted for speeding!

He noticed I was trembling. He was shaking his head, but told me since I was not from that neighborhood and passing through he would let me go without a ticket. I thanked him and said in parting to him that I had only received one speeding ticket in my life...over fifty years ago. Sternly, the policeman said, "Be more careful! Stop and look both ways!" as he returned to his patrol car. I had much to contemplate as I sat quietly for awhile in that restaurant. And then drove on home... carefully!

Proverbs 3:11-12, *do not despise God's reprimand or let it discourage you, for God's discipline is a sign of divine love, the way a parent corrects a beloved child.*

-23-

All that glitters is not gold!

My name is Margie. Let me share a "revelation" that has been lots of help to me since I was about twelve years old. One day as I came home from school my mother was still hosting a few of her lady friends at her monthly, sometimes weekly, tea party. I always loved them because most of the time she would serve my very favorite own homemade cake, apple cream layered cake. I would make a bee-line to the kitchen in hopes of finding some of the cake left over. Most of the time there was. What a joy!

As I was taking my first bite I heard one of the ladies say, "I guess you all have heared that **** is engaged to be married to ****. I just don't see how she could marry someone so bad looking!" Then, another lady said, "Well, look at ****, she married ****, by far the ugliest man I've ever seen. But we all know what a wonderful couple they are; fine looking children, and probably the happiest family in town!" Another lady said, "Looks aren't everything.

Thoughtfulness, being fun-loving, being kind and not being conceited are far better qualities in choosing a marriage partner than good looks!" Then the ladies cracked up when one said, "Looks can never make up for bad sex!" Almost a teenager, I had never ever thought I would marry someone "less" than beautiful. But now like a lightning bolt I was amazed at what I overheard. As for me, I would try find a husband with both good looks and good qualities!

Year after year I would remember what I heard at that tea party when it came to sizing up a boyfriend. I married a young man that was pleasant inside and out. And rather attractive! However, what about me? I wasn't exactly as good looking as a Hollywood star; so I would try to concentrate on the "inner qualities" if I intended to keep him mine! I think what really kept him around for all these many years was my frequent use of my mother's recipe for the apple cream layered cake!

-24-

the amazing grace of will power!

My husband, Brenden Kelly, with a heart problem, was nearing his 75th birthday and let me know that he had one thing he would like to do here on earth before the Lord called him home. "Let's go to Ireland! I would like to find out if the Irish Stew over there is half as good as my Grandmother's was!"

The next day I read a report that a walking club in a nearby town was going on a tour to Germany, Switzerland, England and Ireland. We enjoyed walking even though Brenden's doctor had warned him about exerting too much physical stress as his heart condition was becoming a bit of concern. I telephoned the tour group and signed us up even before telling my husband about it, since I was told that the space availability was quickly closing up. I told him about the trip; and when he found out the itinerary included one week in Ireland he was very happy.

His doctor, however, was not so pleased upon hearing the news and recomended we not go. "If I have to die, it would have to be somewhere-- and what better place than on the Emerald Isle and in God's country! And better yet, after having some authentic good 'ole Irish Stew! Let's do it!" he insisted. What a change had come over him during the few weeks we prepared for the trip. We tried to eat "right." We took short daily walks to see what effects walking had on him, and me too. Everything seemed to be coming along fine. It was a great day when we landed in Frankurt, did lots of touring and took part in four or five Walkfests or IVV Wanderungen in various parts of Germany, as well as in Switzerland. We purposely signed up for shorter walks trying to be a bit careful. In Germany there were frequent rest and refreshment stops featuring locally brewed beer, freshly made bratwurst and lots of friendly people to talk with. Most of them could speak surprisingly good English. We were rather ashamed that we could not do the same with German! But with our Irish names they didn't expect us to. For each walk we completed we received a souvenir medallion or plaque showing the place we walked and the date.

We were so grateful that there had been no problems such as rising blood pressure or fatigue during any of the walks. But I knew that Brenden was very determined to make it to Ireland for that Irish Stew! "I want to be good and hungry when I get there." he told me on several occasions. I made sure we rested as often as we possible.

Now it was time to visit England and Ireland. In Liverpool we boarded a ship for the overnight sail across the ocean, arriving after breakfast aboard ship in the Dublin Harbor. The tour guide had already telephoned our hotel well ahead of time telling them our approximate time of arrival. She had also warned the hotel clerk that most every one would want traditional Irish Stew for the noon meal. The clerk told me that most Americans always did; and they would always find it on the menu.

Approaching the shore of Dublin the entire tour group joined Brenden and I as we waved at everyone on the dock as we slowly arrived. One by one we stepped onto our tour bus that was waiting for us. We were heading straight for our hotel where we would be staying for two nights. There would be a Walkfest the next day on the other side of Dublin. But for lunch there would be Irish Stew!

The hotel concierge greeted our group one by one they stepped off the tour bus. But then there came a strange sort of silence. I noticed that Brenden was breathing heavily and was grasping after his heart. The hotel concierge was notified and he told the bus driver there was a medical doctor in the next block and that the bus should go there immediately with Brenden. They would alert the doctor of our coming.

The doctor greeted us and immediately examined Brenden. Within five minutes an ambulance was ordered up to take us to a nearby hospital. The next morning he passed away.

The tour group was in deep shock. They decided that if Brenden could not have Irish Stew, they would not have it either. One member of the tour group said, "I am sure that God had his best Irish cook in heaven, perhaps even Brendan's grandmother, welcome him with a delicious bowl of heavenly Irish Stew!" Brenden was so determined to get to Ireland. He had such great will power. God gave him the grace and the willpower to go on the tour. I thought to myself, and never told the tour group, that God perhaps did not want my husband to have to say, "Well, the Irish Stew here in Ireland was okay, but not nearly as good as my Grandmother's!" That said, let me conclude that God is so merciful. We dealt for so long the anguish of Brenden's poor heart condition. Now he is at peace and no longer in fear.

-25-

when hate turns into love.....

It is amazing those you meet while on vacation. Escaping an especially cold winter I decided to go to Puerto Rico and the tiny pristine island nearby of Vieques. I had been there once before and found the weather delightful as well as the traditional foods and the happy churches. Rather than wading into the ocean or dealing with sun burn, I preferred to enjoy the coffee and ice cream shops of San Juan's Condado district. I left sizable tips because of staying an inordinate time fully involved with a book.

It was early evening midweek while I was enjoying a stroll only to hear some rather rousing music and singing from a Franciscan parish church in the Condado. Curious, I decided to go inside the church where I found a charismatic prayer meeting going on. The church was filled and I squeezed in without being noticed. It did not bother me that I could not understand Spanish. Music was my language and I could feel it if the hymn was in praise of God; or the positiveness of a prayer to God.

The congregation must have been a prayer group for quite some time for they went into scripture reading, praying for one another, silent devotion, singing and praying in tongues. I was surprised they spent such a long time in praying in tongues and interpreting them. As the gathering came to a close I was totally refreshed, shook a few hands and took leave to return to my hotel. However, as I was leaving a young man who had also been in the church greeted me and asked if I could speak English.

He was from New Jersey and asked me "What in the world was going on in there; I saw the priest; but was it Catholic?" I replied that yes it was Catholic, straight from the Bible. And no it was not of this world, it was **out** of this world! After the apostles received the gifts or the power of the Holy Spirit in the Upper Room, the people thought they had been drinking too much. There's a coffee shop around the corner. We can go there and chat about this if want.

Two hours later we concluded our chat. I asked him when was the last time he had talked for so long about the church, the Holy Spirit, speaking in tongues, laying on of hands in prayer, why the music and the singing was so beautiful, and why he hadn't been to such a gathering before. He admitted he had not been going to church very often. I explained that there were probably such groups in New Jersey but maybe God had in mind of introducing you to the ministries of the Holy Spirit tonight at this special parish in Puerto Rico. He wanted to get your attention! He should feel blessed that God had "set him up" to start with the Baptism of the Holy Spirit process in San Juan. He insisted that he was really turned off by "the speaking in tongues stuff and could never do anything like that!"

I answered, "I agree *you* probably couldn't or wouldn't. But, should the Holy Spirit choose to come into you and gift you with His blessings, you would. The Holy Spirit comes into a person for a reason, to be a blessing to you and then to pass the blessing on to someone or to others. Sometimes God has to set you up to receive a spiritual blessing. Once He busts up a person's stony heart, then He gives gifts "save" a person which then are to be used to help others. Think about it, we have been talking for several hours about what you experienced at the Catholic prayer group tonight. When did God ever get your attention like that before?"

"Never!" he answered. Then as we shook hands to leave, which is a form of a blessing or laying on of hands, I asked him if he would try to find such a prayer group when he returned to New Jersey. He thought for a moment and then smiled, "You know I think I just might do that. It sort of got to me. I guess it's like a song you hear for the first time and don't really like it. Then it gets to you and next time you actually love it. Maybe God did get my attention. I have some things I need to ask Him to help me with!"

-26-

another White Dove, sent from above!...

Editor's note: "Gelobt sei Jesu Christi!" began the email greeting from Germany, meaning: "Praised be Jesus Christ!" and the traditional response: "Jetzt und in Ewigkeit!" or: "Now and forever!"...and then both persons conclude together: "Amen!" We continue with our German friend's email:

Vielen dank, many thanks, for the *Journey Into Wisdom* website and your story #5 which brought back the memory that has come to mean so much to me and my associates here in Germany. I hope you can find someone to translate this story that happened to us. A few years back our firm was so happy to have completed the building of a new residential and retirement center for the Schoenstatt Priests near the headquarters of their colleagues, the Schoenstatt Sisters of Vallendar, Germany.

Our firm was so pleased to have received the building contract. We all prayed for God's help in such a big and meaningful constructon project in the rolling hills area called *The Meadows of Zion.* With typical weather interference, it took almost two years to complete the beautiful complex of buildings. We sighed with relief when everything was finished. We said prayers of thanksgiving when the Father Director shared with us that everything had been approved and setting the date for the dedicatory blessing and Mass could now take place.

All our families were present for the day of dedication. The bishops, priests, religious, and laity lined up for the entrance procession that was a sight to see. All of a sudden, as the door of the church was opened there came a White Dove swooping down and landing on top of the entrance door. It was as if the White Dove was welcoming one and all. Knowing what such a dove signifies in the church, I made a big smile! Was God approving what we had built? I needed such a sign to calm my nerves. What a confirmation of faith! When I see such a dove, even many years later now, I say 'thank you Jesus' and automatically smile!

-27-

blessed to be a blessing....

When I was a baby girl about a year old my mother, a South Korean, left me in the entrance foyer of an orphanage in Seoul. After a few months there, one day a nurse picked me up and put me into the arms of a man... not my real father. He was an American soldier stationed in South Korea. Not too long thereafter I was able to meet my new mother, my new father's wife, in America. Actually I had to figure out these details in the years that followed as I grew up in Texas. I was of mixed parentage; and from what I learned many years later about mixed-nationality children in South Korea their plight is most gruesome and often cruelly shunned.

In all my schools in Texas from pre-care, kindergarten and through high school I often noticed mixed-blood children but for the most part they were not treated any I different than I was. I was always treated nicely. By my middle-school years I had figured out I was Korean and that my parents in America were Americans. They told me that my birth mother, a Korean, had an American soldier boyfriend and before they could get married he was transferred back to the U.S. He never contacted her again. My real mother probably feared how I would be treated and decided it would be best to leave me at the orphanage. It was not uncommon for U.S. servicemen to come to the orphanage to arrange for adoptions. The soldier who adopted me was not the one who was my father with my Korean birth mother. This ends my knowledge I have about Korea and those in Korea.

My life in the U.S. When I was in my early twenties I met a young man a few years older than myself. He was what I considered "huge" being that I am barely past five feet tall. A real good looking Texas cowboy! It was only after a year or so that I began to realize that he was very caught up with his own idea of himself. It was from friends that I gradually learned that he was considered by most people to be a "bully." I might not be very "big"--compared to him, but, I figured out that I was quite a bit smarter. I would try to wiggle out of his bossing me around with jokes and clever little comebacks. He wasn't as tough on me as he was with associates and others. Yet, as time went by, I began to wonder. He was getting more unpleasant all the time. I thought to myself would I have to spend the rest of my life with him? Perhaps he would change.

One morning I was driving off from our ranch to go to work. The country road was well paved and marked, including deer crossing signs. As I was driving along I spotted two deer in the middle of the road. I slowed down;

but the deer remained standing still. I figured I could pass them up by driving to the right of them and driving a bit on the shoulder. As I passed them and still on the shoulder from out of nowhere I suddenly hit what might have been a post that I did not see. The car rolled and rolled into a ditch. I was not badly hurt. An oncoming car spotted the accident and alerted the emergency medics. The county sheriff deputy was also notified as well as a wrecker. The car was totaled.

My husband came to the hospital. I was happy to be able to go home the same day. On the way home I was greatly astonished that my husband repeatedly let me know how terrible it was to lose that nice car. Never a mention about me. As usual I just let it pass. There was hardly a week that went by when he would talk about me wrecking that car. Finally I had had enough. Not long thereafter the judge granted our divorce. Even the air was fresher now!

With the help of my parents I enrolled in a cosmetology school to be a hair dresser. It was in that city where I meet the man who is now my present husband. We both appreciate one another. And life has taken a very positive turn. However, there is one thing that I found out from my medical doctor. I am not able to have a baby. While I am always being reassured by my husband that it does not matter; he will just love me all the same. Well, that's fine, but, I often wondered why I was spared and did not die in that car wreck. A friend told me that something would happen, at a time when God wanted it to happen, that I would find purpose and fulfillment. I could only answer, I hope so!

I heard about *The Gabriel Project, Respect for Life Program* at the local Catholic parish. They had a ministry to help ladies take unwanted pregnancies to full term and raise them; or find couples to adopt them. They would help me find a baby to adopt either locally or at the Mother Seton Home in nearby San Antonio or at Marywood in Austin. I had inquired earlier at an adoption agency in San Antonio but the cost was far out of our reach. Then, I read the stories in this website *Journey Into Wisdom Everlasting.* When I read the saying, *"Blessed to be a blessing"* I promised God that I would do my best to be a blessing if He would bless us with a little baby. I will be emailing you as soon the blessing happens. Thank you so much!

-28- ...awaiting your epiphany experience. Put EPIPHANY REPORT in the subject line of your email, or letter, and send to: alterstolz@gmail.com May God bless you to be a blessing!

POSTLUDE....

These stories represent what is happening in the here and now to all sorts of people. We are the handiwork of God...if we let Him. If left to ourselves, without the Sacraments and being in Communion with Jesus, as it says in **1 Corinthians 3:1-4**... will create gossip, argumentation, prevarication or lies, wrangling and contention between egos that show spiritual immaturity. These stories verify that God intervenes in a special and fatherly way in order to bring us into a more Christ-like maturity. Be thankful for God's gift we might receive of Faith, Hope, and Charity or Agape Love... all to increase the measure of our submission to the Decalogue, the Ten Commandments, and then becoming the Beatitudes. (We **do or obey** the Commandants; and then we **become** the Beatitudes. See **Matthew 5: 3-11** and **Luke 6: 20-22**.) These are the amazing experiences that many have had along their unique Journey into Wisdom Everlasting.

The Bible from beginning to end also relates all kinds of examples that God created us, not leaving us orphans or to fend for ourselves, but that our lives be full of joy despite our egos and those of others around us and in the world. The Epiphany stories of the Old and the New Testament will also help us, finally, to be persuaded that by doing God's Will and following His guiding Star, His Son, our journey will be enlightened by the Light of Christ. Each step of our Journey into Wisdom will reveal Christ's truth to be all that much more real in our lives. What is precious in God's eyes is that we appreciate how Jesus came to this earth to acquaint us with His Father and the loving care of the Holy Spirit. This Everlasting Fellowship is the prize at end of the earthly journey. And to think that we might be included!

A good friend after reading these Epiphany stories, much like St. Thomas, said, "They seemed to be made up stories!" Well, that's an opinion and a start! Thomas was a saint in spite of his having to see things for himself. Though being a skeptic he learned to follow the Commandments and became the Beatitudes; in other words, he became Christ-like to the degree he was graced. Never the less Thomas helped to spread God's Kingdom and bring hope to those enslaved by the ways of the world. With God's grace, in the Name of Christ we are obligated to do likewise!

> ***Revel in your love for God,***
>
> ***you whom God has touched!***
>
> ***...Psalm 31:23***

* * * * * * *

from the Proverbs of Solomon ben-David, ruler of Israel, 1:7... *When you stand in awe of YHWH-- that is when you really understand. But to spurn wisdom and instruction is utter foolishness.*

* * * * * * *

THE HAPPY JOURNEY PRAYER

On your journey may God send you a sunbeam to warm you, a moonbeam to encourage you, a guardian angel to protect you, laughter to brighten you, and faithful friends to help you and stand by you. And when you pray, may the good Lord's answer already be on its way! -adapted from a traditional Irish blessing-

* * * * * * *

By the way, *"should anyone ask you the reason for this* <u>hope</u> *of yours, be ever ready to reply."*... **1 Peter 3:15**

About the Author & The St. Frederick Association

Dear Friends, *We thank you for reading this first volume of **JOURNEY INTO WISDOM EVERLASTING**, from **THE EPIPHANIC ARCHIVES*** by Deacon Kenn Knopp. We also thank those who have emailed us their own personal epiphany stories which have affected their lives. As the archives grow we will be selecting additional testimonies to be included in future printed volumes. We will no longer add to the stories on our internet page. They will soon appear in the printed books so that we may raise funds for our outreach projects as listed below.

We have provided these reports free of charge online in hoping they would encourage people to share with us their experiences. The author at 76 years of **spiritual** youth has been in ill health for some time and has had to retire from ministry as a deacon which he began in 1970. At times he is able to work at his computer to assemble these reports. He is most grateful for that. At the same time he has set up an organization to continue this apostolate according to Matthew 28:19 in the future when he is no longer here.

To receive printed copies of **JOURNEY INTO WISDOM EVERLASTING from THE EPIPHANIC ARCHIVES** please send your donation of at least $20 USD per copy, shipping and handling included, to:

"Journey", % St. Frederick Association, 407 Cora St., Fredericksburg Texas 78624 USA

All proceeds will go as directed to: 1) St. Frederick Association, General Fund;
http://www.saint-frederick-association.com

2) The Catholic High School Scholarship Endowment Fund, Gillespie and Kerr Counties of Texas. This fund is presently active and helps with scholarships at Our Lady of the Hills Catholic High School, Kerrville, Texas.

However, funds designated to go for the development of Bishop Frederick High School Prep, a 9-12 and early college program, in Fredericksburg, Texas, will be placed in escrow until it is actually to be developed.

3) St. Frederick Village & Chapel, Retirement Center for Seniors Fund, in Fredericksburg, Texas.

While sites have yet to be chosen, one potential site would make it possible for the new high school prep and the retirement center to be located on the same property. This is a particularly a good time to designate your contribution in honor of someone or an organization. Please consider remembering The St. Frederick Association in your will and your annual tax exempt donations. The application for 501c3 tax exemption is pending.

For references contact the St. Frederick Association, Board of Advisers:

Paul G. Vick, Attorney-at-Law, 6243 IH-10 West, Suite 860, San Antonio TX 78201. Fredericksburg Texas Office: 1-830-998-8425; email: pvicklaw@aol.com.

Nathan D. Quay, AAMS, Financial Advisor, Edward Jones, 1406 E. Main St., Suite 100, Fredericksburg TX 78624. Tel: 1-830-997-2087; email: nathan.quay@edwardjones.com

Willie Gold, Real Estate Specialist, GMAC-Gillespie Reality, 502 E. Main St., Fredericksburg TX 78624; Tel: 1-830-992-0481. Email: willie@fbgliving.com

Linda Christian Winchester, Public Relations, 212, 1302 Losoya, Suite 100, San Antonio TX 78205. Tel: 1-210-886-0064. Email: linda@sanantoniotourism.com

Debra S. Habecker, Advisor, 1302 N. Elm Street, Fredericksburg TX 78624. Tel: 830-456-2116. Email: debrahabecker@hotmail.com

Mary L. Pearson, MA, Advisor, Cultural Anthropology, Gerontology, 9405 Nashville Court, Lubbock TX 79423. Address in Fredericksburg, private. Cell: 830-992-0621.

Melissa Meyer Rockwood, Advisor, Gerontology, email: melissa.rockwood@va.gov;